BREWERIANA
AMERICAN BEER COLLECTIBLES

Kevin Kious & Donald Roussin

SHIRE PUBLICATIONS

Published in Great Britain in 2012 by Shire Publications Ltd, Midland House, West Way, Botley, Oxford OX2 0PH, United Kingdom.

44-02 23rd Street, Suite 219, Long Island City, NY 11101, USA.

E-mail: shire@shirebooks.co.uk   www.shirebooks.co.uk

A CIP catalogue record for this book is available from the British Library.

Shire Library no. 641.   ISBN-13: 978 0 74781 044 5

Kevin Kious and Donald Roussin have asserted their right under the Copyright, Designs and Patents Act, 1988, to be identified as the authors of this book.

Designed by Tony Truscott Designs, Sussex, UK and typeset in Perpetua and Gill Sans.

Printed in China through Worldprint Ltd.

12 13 14 15 16   10 9 8 7 6 5 4 3 2 1

COVER IMAGE
An American icon, Anheuser-Busch has been brewing beer for more than 135 years. As early as 1901, the brewery broke the 1 million-barrel production mark. By the late 1950s, Anheuser-Busch, the brewer of Budweiser, became the nation's largest brewer. (Image courtesy of The Advertising Archives.)

TITLE PAGE IMAGE
Yuengling, of Pottsville, Pennsylvania, still emphasizes in its advertising that it is America's oldest brewery.

CONTENTS PAGE IMAGE
This detailed factory scene tray from Milwaukee includes an image of its beer baron namesake, Joseph Schlitz.

PHOTO CREDITS
All images courtesy of the authors unless otherwise stated

CONTENTS

INTRODUCTION

BEER. The widely popular beverage, made primarily from water, grain, hops, and yeast has been around for thousands of years. From its crude beginnings in the ancient Middle East, brewing beer has become a huge, worldwide industry. The collecting of items associated with the brewing of beer, however, is of much more recent origin.

"Breweriana" is a term used to describe the many types of collectable items related to beer. The term was coined in 1969 by author and breweriana collector Will Anderson. He had just published his first book, *Anderson's Turn-of-the-Century Brewery Directory*, and was seeking a term that could be used to encompass all forms of "beer stuff." While driving home one day from his job at *Reader's Digest*, breweriana popped into Anderson's head. Although some still have difficulty pronouncing it (the correct way is simply to say "brewery-Anna"), the term has stuck. Anderson titled his next book *Beers, Breweries, and Breweriana*.

The variety of breweriana items is astounding. Brewers have placed their names on an incredible number of surfaces. Many of these items are utilitarian: bottles, cans, coasters, napkins, and matchbooks. Others are ornate: lithographs, etched glasses, reverse-painted images on glass, fine china, and porcelain signs. Some are bizarre: condoms, combs, golf tees, neckties, and foam scrapers.

Not long after Anderson coined the term, the hobby of collecting breweriana exploded in popularity. Due to the huge number of items available, today's enthusiasts can choose collecting specialties

Children often were depicted in pre-Prohibition advertising. A colorful example is this Stroh's tray, from Detroit.

that not only match their personal tastes and their display areas, but also their budgets, whether large or small.

    This book seeks to explore the many forms of breweriana and tie them into the history of brewing. The journey starts with the invention of beer and shows no sign of abating.

Below left:
A tip tray from Goebel of Detroit, Michigan, probably meant for use as a coaster.

Above right:
Utilitarian items like this purse mirror from the Cape Brewery of Cape Girardeau, Missouri, kept the company's name in front of the lady of the house—and the women who ordered beer deliveries for the home.

"It's tasty" is the message from the beer-drinking bear pictured on this tray from Mathie Brewing of Los Angeles.

THE NEIGHBORHOOD BREWERY

EXACTLY when the first beer advertisement appeared is uncertain, but it is doubtful that early brewers concerned themselves much with such matters. They were too busy performing the arduous task of making beer.

For centuries, brewing was primarily a household duty, usually performed by women, diminutively referred to in the English vernacular as "brewsters." Commercial breweries were established gradually, but until 1870 or so, they simply weren't very worried about distinguishing themselves from their competitors, except maybe when it came to brewing better beer.

Early tavern advertising consisted primarily of ale stakes, which were poles hung outside of taverns to indicate that beer was available inside. Such signage dates at least to fourteenth-century England, when laws were passed limiting their length to seven feet. At some taverns, ale stakes were decorated; at others, just a broom was used.

Newspaper ads were the primary way early nineteenth-century breweries announced themselves to prospective patrons, although wooden sign boards for ale and porter began appearing in England in the early 1800s. A period English engraving shows a pair of such tavern signs, one for H. Meux and Co.'s Entire, the other for Goding's XXX Ale. Some posters were used by brewers during this period as well.

In the antebellum United States, brewers in cities were mostly content to serve their neighborhoods. Breweries also sprang up in many small towns. In any village that had at least a hundred German immigrants, it was likely that at least one of them was brewing beer. While the Germans and their lager beer would grow to dominate the nation's brewing industry, many English ale brewers set up shop as

As simple as it gets: a block print depicting an ale stake advertising sign affixed onto a tavern, in 1400s England. (From *One Hundred Years of Brewing*, H. S. Rich & Co; 1903.)

well. Brewers in small towns and large cities alike, unless they were on a railroad line or navigable river, were restricted to expanding their market as far as a horse, driver, and wagon could venture from and return to the brewery in a day.

Thus, despite the huge number of breweries in America by 1860 (it has been estimated that there were more than twelve hundred), no breweriana exists for most of them. Neighborhood breweries saw little need to advertise, and any cooperage or equipment they used, even if it has survived, typically bears no inscription.

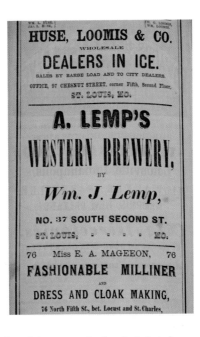

Directory ads, like this 1858 example from Adam Lemp, St. Louis, are some of the few breweriana items from this period that can still be found.

Most 1840s-era advertising, as represented by this trade card from the Ohm & Keine brewery in Germany, was printed in black ink on white stock.

An exception to this is found with brewers who bottled their beer. Although beer was being bottled as early as the 1500s, bottles were so

7

difficult to obtain that they were considered a luxury. But by the 1850s, more brewers were bottling, and they used bottles embossed with their names. Indeed, bottles still can be found for some brewers for which there is no other evidence of their existence. The use of embossed bottles was not necessarily seen by these breweries as a form of advertising. Instead, it mainly was intended to aid them in getting their bottles back from customers.

Advertisements for pre-1870 brewers also appear in a few other places, including early city directory ads. Other ephemera found for these breweries include letterhead, bills of sale, keg tags, business records, and even personal diaries kept by a few brewers. But most items from this era are extremely rare. While this makes them valuable to collectors, their esoteric nature can make them a bargain when compared to some newer items.

As industrialization began hitting the brewing industry full-force in the 1870s, changes that revolutionized the industry also would result in the production of breweriana. Both the beer business and brewery advertising were ready to enter a golden age.

Opposite:
A nice selection of Anheuser-Busch, St. Louis, embossed branch bottles, from its coast-to-coast depot network.

A thermometer issued by Bergner & Engel Brewing, of Philadelphia, advertising Tannhaeuser, the name of a famous Richard Wagner opera.

9

BEER BARONS AND INDUSTRIALIZATION

B Y 1873, more than four thousand breweries were operating in the United States. Most were small concerns producing and packaging kegged beer for a local clientele. The brewing process itself was restricted to the cooler months, the beer was aged and stored in underground cellars, and any other refrigeration consisted of storing ice cut during the winter and packed in straw. But numerous inventions soon were to begin dramatically changing the brewing industry.

The most important changes involved mechanization within the brewery, as the process went from one that was little understood to one that was somewhat scientific. Advances in glass production and the development of pasteurization led to greater availability of beer in bottles. Improvements in equipment enabled bottling to evolve from a manual to a highly mechanized process.

An improved transportation system allowed brewers who were so inclined to expand their export business. The great expansion of railroads gave breweries a chance to ship their products long distances, using icehouses and storage depots strategically located along the tracks. Some of the larger breweries shipped so much beer that they owned their own rail cars.

The shipping business proved to be especially lucrative for breweries in the midwestern cities of Milwaukee, Wisconsin, and St. Louis, Missouri. Located where the population was less dense and with many local competitors, their method of growth was to invade the more populous East as well as the South and West, where there were fewer breweries. Pabst and Schlitz of Milwaukee, Lemp and Anheuser-Busch of St. Louis, and, to a lesser extent, many others, sent their beer across the country and all over the world.

The late 1870s also saw the introduction of refrigeration into breweries. Although initially unreliable, refrigerating machines were quickly improved. This not only allowed breweries to make beer year-round, it also enabled them to more closely control the brewing process.

A rough economy chased many brewers out of business around 1880, and economies of scale enjoyed by some of the large companies led to heated competition between small local breweries and out-of-town giants. As a way to

Opposite:
To catch a man's eye in a tavern, feature a pretty woman in the ad. Surely that was the strategy behind this 1908 calendar from Cape Brewery & Ice, Cape Girardeau, Missouri.

Above: Around 1900, the Val Blatz brewery of Milwaukee provided this tour booklet as a gift to visitors of its plant.

Right: Lemp of St. Louis was an early shipping brewery. This tin sign shows eight different brands of "The Choicest Product of the Brewer's Art."

Right: This "girl in the pink dress" self-framed tin sign was issued by Anheuser-Busch of St. Louis to promote its flagship brew, Budweiser.

Far right: An early Budweiser tin sign on wood. The sign's approximate age can be determined in that the bottle is sealed by a bailed cork stopper.

distinguish themselves from their competitors the brewers began thinking about ways to promote their product. To help simplify their marketing efforts, branding became popular. Most breweries continued producing a variety of beer styles, but eventually concentrated on a single brand or two. For example, Pabst and Schlitz chose eponymous names for their leading brands, while Lemp borrowed the Falstaff name from Shakespeare. Budweiser became the flagship label of Anheuser-Busch. Originally the name was associated with a beer style brewed by numerous breweries. Anheuser-Busch had started brewing it in 1876 as a "contract brand" for liquor dealer Carl Conrad. Following Conrad's bankruptcy and a series of successful trademark lawsuits, the St. Louis brewer became the almost exclusive American brewer of the brand.

Though the vast majority of beer produced was still being put into wooden kegs (typically branded with the brewery name), bottling continued to grow in popularity even for most small breweries. Corks had been the primary

stoppers used for beer bottles prior to the 1870s. Many breweries made advertising corkscrews for these bottles. The number of other stoppers invented for bottles was staggering. The "Lightning stopper," the name commonly given to a seal patented in 1875 by Charles De Quillfeldt, consisted of a wire-attached, swing-away rubber gasket that became popular among breweries. The "Lightning" name was borrowed from the trademarked "Lightning" brand fruit jars developed by Henry Putnam. The "Hutter stopper" came around in 1893. Karl Hutter had acquired the rights to the "Lightning" stopper and patented his namesake improvement. It featured a cone-shaped porcelain stopper with

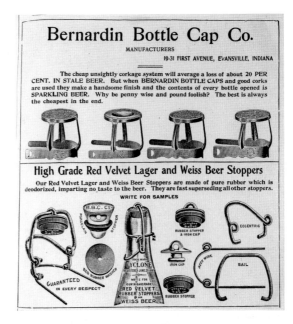

a washer on the end. Advances in printing technology allowed brewers the opportunity to decorate these stoppers with their names and emblems.

This 1912 ad from Bernardin Company of Evansville, Indiana, from *The Western Brewer*, illustrates but a few of the hundreds of stopper designs patented by World War I.

Stoppers gradually were replaced by the "crown cap" developed in 1892 by William Painter. It consisted of a single-use, metal top featuring a flanged edge with a cork and paper lining inside. Its effectiveness and popularity led to the standardization of bottles and bottling machinery by 1920. Today's crowns are little changed (except for the use of cork ending in the 1960s), and they continue to be highly collectible.

By the early twentieth century, most breweries were still using embossed bottles, although labels were being glued to many of them. Beginning in the 1840s, breweries had begun using simple black-and-white labels; the use of fancier labels with striking colors and graphics increased dramatically in the 1880s and 1890s. Some brewers used die-cut labels of a variety of shapes and sizes.

Brewers typically shipped these bottles in wooden boxes with the brewery name inked onto them. Some of these boxes were designed to fit as many as three cases of beer—a heavy load when full, especially considering the thickness of the bottles.

A crown cap from Griesedieck Beverage of St. Louis. The name "Hek" was inspired by an ancient Egyptian malt beverage.

An early, simply designed label, printed in only two colors, from Kurth Brewing, Columbus, Wisconsin.

Breweries usually had taverns and beer gardens on their grounds. Most of them also went into the saloon business. In fact, a key to success in the U.S. brewing industry before Prohibition was the so-called "tied house." These were saloons owned by a brewery, typically leased out to an operator who then was obliged to serve only the owner's products. Many of the shipping breweries like Pabst, Schlitz, and Anheuser-Busch established tied houses all over the country. Often even the chairs and other fixtures in the taverns were

A delivery wagon plaster wall hanger that carries the name of another beer baron, Jacob Ruppert, of New York City.

provided by the brewery, some of them emblazoned with its name.

By controlling retail and wholesale outlets alike, successful brewery owners were able to amass large fortunes. The term "beer baron" is, indeed, an apt description of these industrial giants. Baronial mansions and trips around the world were typical of the lifestyle of the owners of successful breweries.

The first generation of beer barons was predominantly German immigrants. Although many were trained brewers, others came from varied backgrounds. Theodore Hamm of St. Paul, Minnesota, was a butcher before he took over a failing brewery in 1864. Adolphus Busch hailed from a brewing family and became a partner with father-in-law Eberhard Anheuser, who in 1860 acquired a small St. Louis brewery that had been founded in the early 1850s. Gustav Pabst likewise married into the beer business, following a career as a ship captain. In 1864, he became co-owner of a brewery founded twenty years earlier by his in-laws.

Fellow Milwaukee resident Joseph Schlitz began in the beer business as a bookkeeper for August Krug. He took over management of the brewery after Krug's death in the 1850s, and later married his widow. The business was incorporated in 1874 as the Joseph Schlitz Brewing Company. Following Schlitz's death the next year, in a shipwreck while returning from a trip to Germany, control of the brewery passed to his wife and her nephews, the Uihlein brothers.

Other beer barons included the Rupperts of New York. Jacob Ruppert was a German immigrant from a family of brewers and struck out on his own in 1867. His son, Jacob Jr., followed in his footsteps and took over the business following his father's death in 1915. The son became co-owner of the New York Yankees baseball team that same year, a role that kept him busy during the dry years of Prohibition, after which the brewery reopened and persisted until 1965.

An earlier New York beer baron was Matthew Vassar of Poughkeepsie. Born in 1792 in Norfolk County, England, Vassar came to the United States in 1796 with his parents. His father James farmed in Dutchess County, New York, for a few years before moving to the

Stylized tin signs, like this Amber Ale from Feigenspan, of Newark, New Jersey, were issued by many breweries around 1900; "P.O.N." stands for "Pride of Newark."

In the early 1900s, most taverns had a metal corner sign mounted at the front entrance, like this rare one from the Klausmann Brewery, in St. Louis.

15

county seat of Poughkeepsie to operate an ale brewery. At age fifteen, Matthew ran away from home to avoid an apprenticeship with a tanner. He returned three years later to work at the brewery.

The Vassar brewery was destroyed by fire in 1811, killing Matthew's brother. His father returned to farming, but Matthew continued brewing at a different location. A new brewery was built in 1815, and it became hugely successful. Vassar was an early shipping brewery, forging a reputation for "Poughkeepsie ale" throughout the West. Vassar helped found the college that bears his name in 1865. The brewery closed in 1896; Vassar died years earlier, in 1868, while delivering a farewell speech to the Vassar College Board of Trustees. The school is still going strong.

These brewers and others became household names both during their lifetimes, as they steered their companies to prominence, and beyond. Many of them had egos as big as their mansions, so it's no wonder they were enthusiastic about advertising their namesake products. A few even used their own images on some of their advertising, ranging from a tray featuring Detroit, Michigan, brewer Frank Zynda to peepholes in pocket knives that showed the image of Adolphus Busch.

Outdoor photographs of pre-Prohibition taverns owned by these beer barons tend to show a wealth of brewery advertising and are a highly collectible form of breweriana. They usually include metal corner signs shaped to be tucked neatly on a building's corners. Similar signs were designed to hang on flat surfaces. Those saloons not owned by breweries often displayed such outdoor signage from two or more breweries. Although thousands of these colorful signs were made, surprisingly few of them survive today.

The advertising and novelty industry rose to the demands of the brewers by manufacturing a huge array of interesting and often colorful display pieces. Innovations in technology were not exclusive to the brewing industry, and advances in various production processes resulted in the availability of nifty new advertising items.

Porcelain signs, made by fusing ground glass crystals onto a sheet of iron, became a popular form of advertising. At least one manufacturer guaranteed these signs not to fade, rust, peel, or tarnish for ten years. Efforts also were made to design illuminated outdoor signs. These included "swing drum" signs designed to hang on a pole and burn oil or kerosene. Many breweries used these

Not all corner signs were tin. This great example, from the Evansville Brewing Association of Evansville, Indiana, is made of porcelain.

signs, which derived their name from their bass-drum shape, and possibly because they were supposed to "drum up" business, but practically none of them survives, likely because of damage caused by the fuel, plus their fragility and large size.

The inside of the typical saloon featured other forms of brewery advertising. Improvements in color printing from the 1880s onward led to commercial artists producing spectacular illustrations for the brewers. Many of these were so-called "factory scenes," featuring the brewery's buildings (sometimes including structures that didn't exist) in their glorious industrial splendor, with the obligatory smoke pouring from the stacks.

The annual production of bock-style beer, typically available beginning every year in May, also gave breweries a reason to produce colorful lithographs. Some of the bock posters are truly spectacular, with bold colors and imaginative designs. Most feature billy goats, the symbol of bock beer. The story of how bock-style beer, brewed using darker malt, was named is the stuff of many tall tales. The simplest and most logical explanation comes from the fact that the beer originally was brought into Munich by the brewers from nearby Einbock. This was shortened to just "bock," the German word for a male goat—and an irresistible advertising symbol. Some advertising artists chose to put the goats in laughable situations; others featured Gambrinus, the mythical Flemish king associated with beer brewing. These signs are highly sought by collectors.

Reverse-on-glass signs also were popular with breweries around the turn of the twentieth century. These colorful

Some trays, mostly from New England breweries, also were fabricated in porcelain. Chief Skenandoah dominates this offering from Oneida Brewing, Utica, New York.

Certainly an eye-catcher, this fanciful bock beer sign was issued by Christian Moerlein of Cincinnati, Ohio.

A reverse-on-glass (or an "R-O-G," as some collectors call them), from the American Brewing Company, St. Louis.

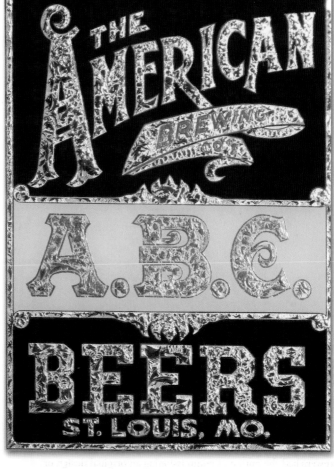

A typical pre-Prohibition, acid-etched glass, this one distributed by E. Porter Brewing, Joliet, Illinois.

decorations consisted of a piece of glass painted on the back. Some had a cardboard backing, while others were designed to be framed. The artwork on some of these signs still dazzles.

Patrons sitting in a tavern are apt to spend considerable time looking at the glass out of which they are drinking. Thus, many brewers large and small opted to have their names etched into drinking glasses. The introduction of mold-pressed glass allowed for the production of inexpensive thin-shelled glasses for this purpose. The many different shapes and sizes used suggest a wide variety of manufacturers.

The designs were acid-etched onto the glass using a silk-screen process. Some used color, but most did not. Although easy to break, a lot of them have survived. Part of the reason for this may rest in the fact that these glasses

The caption on the bottom of this oval National Lager tray, provided by National Brewing of San Francisco, reads "Pastimes on the Frontier."

represented an early brewery collectible. They often were placed in a cabinet at home rather than used in a saloon.

Heavier embossed glasses, mugs, and steins also were popular advertising media for breweries. Some of these vessels were used in restaurants and in beer gardens, which commonly operated on the grounds of many breweries.

Also manufactured for both home and tavern use were trays. Metal trays with designs engraved upon them were the first to be used by brewers. The first printed metal trays were made in 1895 by the Tuscarora Company of Coshocton, Ohio. Other manufacturers soon followed. Brewers had the option of commissioning an original design or using a "stock" tray that used a standard design to which the brewery name (or design elements like bottles) could be added.

One style of these trays was the smaller, so-called "tip" tray. Though some of them may have been used for the placement of servers' tips, most probably were used as coasters. Others were consigned for use as ashtrays.

Larger trays were issued in various shapes and designs. Women were a popular subject, as were scenes that featured labels and bottles of the brewery's various products. Jumbo-sized trays known as "chargers" also were produced. Their

This tip tray, distributed by the Columbus Brewing, of Columbus, Ohio, has in its center a portrait of (who else?) Christopher Columbus.

A colorful celluloid match safe. John B. Busch was an older brewing brother of Adolphus, the latter of Anheuser-Busch fame.

elaborate designs suggest they were meant to hang on a wall rather than to lug food around.

Breweries also used a wide variety of other items for advertising in the early 1900s. Many produced calendars designed both to hang in taverns and for customers to take home. Popular themes included pretty women—still quite popular in brewery advertising—and children, whose association with alcohol is unacceptable in today's society.

Match safes, small containers for keeping one's matches dry and tidy, were common brewery giveaways and were made of both metal and celluloid. Paper matchbooks came into use in the 1890s, and breweries also latched onto them as an advertising device. Although they were disposable, most breweries considered matchbooks a highly suitable advertising medium. In 1902, the Pabst Brewing Company ordered 10 million matchbooks from the Diamond Match Company.

Cardboard coasters also came into use before Prohibition, coming to the United States around 1900 from Germany. They quaintly became known as "mats" in Great Britain. The aim of these disposable wood-pulp coasters was simple: to soak up spilled beer and condensation dripping from glasses.

Cardboard coasters are inexpensive, which is why Lebanon Valley Brewing, of Lebanon, Pennsylvania, and hundreds of other brewers have favored them for advertising.

Invented last but surely not least in the eyes of collectors are the pre-Prohibition signs known as "Vitrolites." Made using the "decalcolamia" transfer process, they were invented by the Meyercord Company of Chicago in the early 1900s. Meyercord contracted with the Opalite Tile Company of Pennsylvania to manufacture signs using decals. It later discovered that Opalite was buying the decals from a German company. In 1908, Meyercord and some Opalite officials formed a new company called Meyercord-Carter to build a factory in Vienna, West Virginia, and began producing Vitrolite signs. The firm was reorganized and incorporated as The Vitrolite Company in 1910.

Glass Vitrolites, like this pristine sign from Walter Brewing of Eau Claire, Wisconsin, are highly prized by many breweriana collectors.

Vitrolite advertised its design process in period brewing industry publications as a "quick way for applying your advertising message permanently to wood, glass, metal, or leather." The company's first decal signs were made to be applied directly to windows, but they soon were being put on signs made of glass with black and milk-white bodies burned into the surface. A testament to the effectiveness of this process is still-existing Vitrolites, which often are as beautiful today as they were when new.

Vitrolites often were designed to be illuminated from within. They ended up being produced for breweries for not much more than a decade, killed by Prohibition and, just like many breweries, destined not to return.

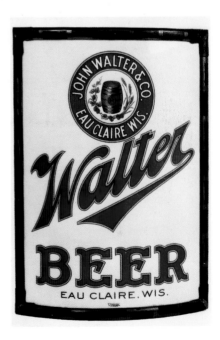

WHAT'LL WE DO ON A SATURDAY NIGHT
(WHEN THE TOWN GOES DRY)
by Harry Ruby

THE DRY YEARS

THE BREWING INDUSTRY in the United States entered the twentieth century in fine fettle. Captains within the business marked their triumphs with the 1903 publication of the massive book *100 Years of Brewing*. This elaborate tome (priced at $25 postage paid, a tidy sum at the time) delivered the history of brewing throughout the world and over the ages, with a special emphasis on the development of brewing in North America.

To the U.S. brewers who cracked open this book upon its arrival in the mail, it had to have been unfathomable that within twenty years of its publication the industry it chronicled would be declared illegal.

Prohibitionists had begun making their influence felt early in the days of the republic. "Local option" laws were passed as early as 1829, and Maine had been first to pass a statewide prohibition law, in 1851. But the movement had waxed and waned, so by 1904, only three states were dry.

Led by the Anti-Saloon League of America, the movement gained strength soon thereafter. States and cities once more began voting themselves dry, putting a considerable crimp in beer sales. Aided by the anti-German sentiment brought about by World War I and abetted by material conservation measures put in place by the federal government, it was a crippled brewing industry that was outlawed with the passage of the 18th Amendment. The law was ratified on January 16, 1919, and was scheduled to become effective one year later.

In response to national prohibition, many breweries simply closed their doors, never to reopen. Employees of the large Lemp Brewing Company in St. Louis learned of its closing shortly before the law took effect. They showed up for work one day to find the entrances padlocked shut. The buildings soon were sold to a shoe company. The Christian Moerlein Brewing Company in Cincinnati was the largest in brewery-rich Ohio. It closed in 1919 and never came back, although a small brewery called the Old Munich Brewing Company operated out of some of its buildings during the 1930s.

Other breweries continued during Prohibition by producing nonalcoholic beverages like soft drinks and "near beer" (in regard to the latter,

Opposite:
Buyers of Tin Pan Alley sheet music like this one could express their views about Prohibition in song. Most songs of the genre lamented the enactment of the 18th Amendment.

Like many other breweries, Falstaff in St. Louis tried its hand at selling root beer during Prohibition, after the brewing of real beer was banned.

A lapel pin back button supporting the "dry" movement in Ohio.

A Goetz Country Club near-beer bottle from 1925. It sold well because it spiked well with alcohol. From the Goetz brewery in St. Joseph, Missouri.

it was indeed a sage who said that whoever gave it the name was a damned poor judge of distance). Although a few brewers succeeded at the alternative beverage business, sales for most were anemic. A number of breweries diversified into other products, again with limited success. The Pabst Brewing Company branched into the cheese business, while Anheuser-Busch kept its doors open by selling yeast.

One brewery actually thrived during Prohibition. The M. K. Goetz Brewing Company of St. Joseph, Missouri, had considerable experience in brewing nonintoxicating beer in the years leading up to 1920. Its Country Club brand, introduced as a regular beer in 1898, was selected as the label that would carry the company's near-beer hopes during the 1920s. Country Club was brewed using a revolutionary method of removing the alcohol and was designed to have a flavor that went well with black-market grain alcohol. The resulting product met with such success that the brewery prospered during Prohibition. While some breweries were crumbling into disrepair, the Goetz plant ended up ten times its former size.

One other survival strategy kept some breweries alive: bootlegging. A substantial

Although it was illegal to brew beer during Prohibition, selling the raw ingredients wasn't. Many breweries, like Schlitz of Milwaukee, sold malt syrup, sometimes jokingly labeled "for baking use only."

number of brewers continued making beer illegally. All it took was a near-beer permit (or not) and a willingness to fail to remove the alcohol from the real beer needed to produce the fake stuff. Most of the outlaw breweries eventually were caught and put out of business. They included brewers large (Wiedemann of Newport, Kentucky) and small (Mascoutah Brewing Company of Mascoutah, Illinois), but a few succeeded in marketing beer for the duration of Prohibition. One was the Old Appleton Brewing and Ice Company of Old Appleton, Missouri. Despite several scrapes with the law, it made and sold beer throughout the dry years. One ploy it used to keep from getting caught was to put fake Canadian labels on its bottled beer.

This label may read "Ontario" (Canada), to fool the Feds, but it was printed locally and then applied onto bootleg bottles of beer by the brewery in Old Appleton, Missouri.

Certainly the items produced by breweries during Prohibition for their various products can be considered breweriana, but the 1920–32 era serves mainly as a handy dividing line for collectors, marking the difference between those items produced before Prohibition (pre-Pro) and those made after (post-Pro).

Sentiment in favor of Prohibition was unraveling quickly by 1930, and the election of Franklin Delano Roosevelt in 1932 as U.S. President ensured its demise. The brewers were even given a favor: in advance of the presumed ratification of the 21st Amendment repealing Prohibition, low-alcohol beer was declared nonintoxicating and could be sold to the public starting on April 7, 1933.

The Schott Brewing Company of Highland, Illinois, honored Franklin Delano Roosevelt in the early 1930s by issuing this flattering bust of the president. (Courtesy of George Baley.)

25

BEER IS BACK

WHEN BEER became legal again in the United States upon the stroke of midnight on "New Beer's Eve," fewer than fifty breweries had beer ready to answer the first call. For a while these companies could quickly sell all the beer they could make, but within a couple years, there were hundreds of competitors.

By the time the 21st Amendment was passed, the country was mired in economic depression, and although a lot of capitalists were eager to get in the business, it would take many years for beer consumption to reach pre-Prohibition levels.

Much had changed in the world during the thirteen years of national Prohibition. Advances in transportation meant that breweries wouldn't need horse stables any more. Wooden kegs would be replaced by steel and aluminum, and while wooden bottle cases hung on for more than a decade, they were destined to be replaced by cardboard (which itself has become nearly obsolete).

Perhaps most significantly, the tastes of the American public had changed when it came to beverages. Lager beer had become king in the United States well before Prohibition, and many breweries had begun producing "extra pale lagers" in the decades leading up to it. But darker, maltier beers were still the order of the day before 1920. This is evident from brewery worker photos taken during the pre-Prohibition era. When the employees posed with glasses of beer in their hands, invariably the beer was dark in color.

However, during the dark days, the public had grown used to sweeter beverages like soft drinks. Scofflaw drinkers grew used to the sugary mixers used to flavor bootleg drinks. In response to demand, post-Prohibition brewers had to choose: They could either produce a less flavorful beverage or else suffer poor sales. Although many breweries continued making a number of different beer styles, most soon settled on a pale pilsner-style beer. Only some breweries, primarily in the eastern United States, would bother to make the top-fermenting, more heavily hopped ales any longer.

Opposite:
The Schorr-Kolkschneider Brewing Company of St. Louis, Missouri, welcomed Repeal by ordering a new fleet of delivery trucks. (Courtesy Jim Siegel).

A metal keg from the small Warsaw Brewing, of Warsaw, Illinois. The brewery was erected with a commanding view of the nearby Mississippi River.

This 1934 postcard featuring the Peerless Brewing plant in Washington, Missouri, stressed that its Cardinal beer was "fully aged"—in contrast to the cheap "green" bootleg beer often sold during Prohibition.

Thirsty beer drinkers didn't seem to mind. They were just happy to have a beer in their hands. And although their products' flavor may have been slightly diminished, the brewers' zeal to advertise certainly wasn't. Some of the mainstay advertising items of the pre-Prohibition era came back, and modern technology quickly added exciting new items upon which breweries could display their names and into which they could package their products.

One of the more profound developments was the use of cans for packaging beer. Can companies and a few brewers had toyed with the idea of canned beer prior to Prohibition. They encountered problems with the beer reacting with the metal in the can. But a lining called "vinylite," created by the Union Carbide Company, eventually solved this problem. This synthetic resin was used as a coating on the inside of the can, preventing the liquid from ever coming into contact with the metal.

The Krueger Brewing Company of Newark, New Jersey, was the first to market beer in cans. American Can Company had made them an offer they couldn't refuse, installing the canning line and providing the cans free

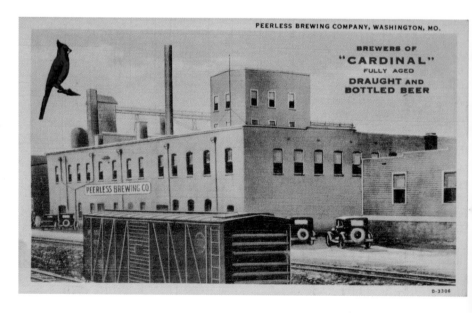

PEERLESS BREWING COMPANY, WASHINGTON, MO.

BREWERS OF
"CARDINAL"
FULLY AGED
DRAUGHT AND
BOTTLED BEER

PEERLESS BREWING CO

D-3306

of charge. A two thousand-can test run in 1933 was distributed to employees and friends of the brewery. The results were satisfactory, but the can company took another year improving the welding on the seam of the can. It also spent that time settling on a combination of vinylite and enamel to coat the inside of its "keglined" cans.

It wasn't until January 1935 that cans were marketed to the general public. Krueger chose to can both beer and ale, and Richmond, Virginia, an outlier of the company's distribution area, was chosen as the test market.

Sales were brisk enough that numerous other brewers soon began canning their beverages. Within a year, nearly forty breweries were using cans. Some were using cans made by rival canning company Continental Can, which had developed an alternate design: a can with a cone-shaped top and lid sealed with a crown just like those used for bottles.

A standard opener could be used for these "Cap-Sealed" cans, but a different style of opener had to be designed for use with American's flat-top cans. This gave rise to the style of opener that somehow acquired the nickname "church key." Savvy beer drinkers soon were carrying openers that could be used for either bottles or cans.

Sales of canned beer took off, aided by the increasing consumption of beer at home, spurred by the spread of household refrigerators. Still, by 1940, with almost five hundred breweries canning their beer, cans accounted for only 10 percent of total beer sales.

Cans weren't the only new form of breweriana appearing after Prohibition. Another came about due to regulatory changes mandating a three-tiered system of beer distribution in the United

Krueger Brewing of Newark, New Jersey, hawked the merits of the company's newfangled beer cans, when they were first placed on the market in 1934.

Schlitz Brewing of Milwaukee distributed this easel-back cardboard sign cleverly die-cut in the shape of its new "Cap-Sealed" cone-top beer cans.

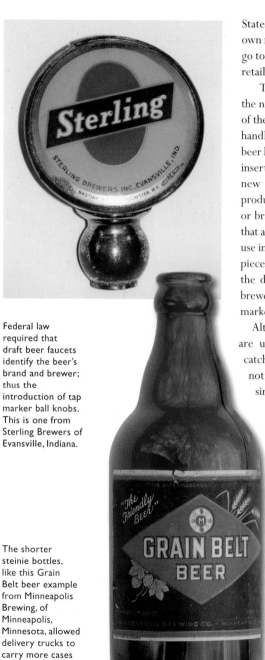

Federal law required that draft beer faucets identify the beer's brand and brewer; thus the introduction of tap marker ball knobs. This is one from Sterling Brewers of Evansville, Indiana.

The shorter steinie bottles, like this Grain Belt beer example from Minneapolis Brewing, of Minneapolis, Minnesota, allowed delivery trucks to carry more cases of beer on every trip.

States. Brewers no longer were permitted to own retail establishments. Their product had to go to a distributor, who then delivered it to the retailer. The tied house was dead.

The law also mandated that taverns display the names of the beer brands being served out of their draft beer taps. Before Prohibition, the handles used by bartenders to dispense draft beer had gone unadorned except for decorative inserts made of ebonite or other materials. The new regulation opened up a market in producing tap markers displaying the brewery or brand names. It was around this same time that a similar device, the "pump clip," came into use in Britain. Pump clips were attached with a piece of metal that literally was clipped onto the dispenser rather than screwed in. Some breweries in the United States used this style of marker as well.

Although twenty-first-century beer drinkers are used to seeing a huge variety of eye-catching tap knobs, brewers in the 1930s did not see them primarily as advertising pieces, since the early ones were small and tended to be round or oval. One popular style was the classic "ball" knob, consisting of a chrome-plated metal body with a porcelain or enamel inlaid disc. Similar knobs were made of brass-lined Bakelite.

Even if these early tap knobs weren't used as advertising tools, marketing was still seen as quite important. The reopened breweries used many of the same types of advertising devices they had used prior to Prohibition. Reverse-on-glass signs, paper and cardboard posters, coasters, and matchbooks were still popular. Glassware was back, although etched glassware was almost gone, replaced by enamel paint sprayed on vessels of a huge variety of shapes and sizes.

Space-saving bottles called "stubbies" and "steinies" also were new to the scene. By government mandate, their labels, like those of all other bottles and cans, bore the statement "internal revenue tax paid." In the early-to mid-1930s, these bottles also displayed the "U-permit" designation, a number assigned to each brewery by the federal government, which had to appear on labels until 1935.

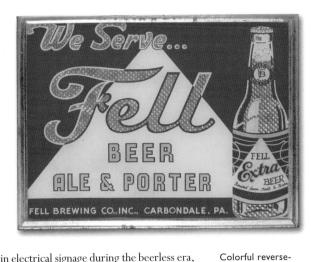

Colorful reverse-on-glass signs, like this from Fell Brewing, of Carbondale, Pennsylvania, were issued by many small breweries during the 1930s.

Advances also had been made in electrical signage during the beerless era, and brewers were quick to take advantage of them. Neons could be displayed both indoors and out, and fancy lights were produced using a variety of imaginative designs and with great names like "bullet" and "cab." Bullet signs were actually shaped like a bullet and lit from the inside or behind, while the shape of cab lights mimicked those of the signs found on the roof of a taxi. Bright colors and motion effects were achieved using a variety of interesting motorized devices including internal parts that spun and rotated and liquid-filled tubes that bubbled when heated. Colorful outdoor and indoor metal signs of all shapes and sizes continued to be used by many breweries as well.

The post-Prohibition beer business was to become highly competitive. Many underfinanced breweries quickly went out of business. Items produced

Four-color neon signs were still expensive to produce at the time that the Ballantine Brewing Company of Newark, New Jersey, issued this one.

by them are among the most sought after by modern enthusiasts. The record
is unclear as to which was the first reopened U.S. brewery to fail and close
its doors. But the title of the first beer can to be obsolete clearly goes to
Kent Ale, an India Pale Ale-style of beer issued by the pioneering Krueger
brewery. It was canned for only a few months beginning late in 1935.

Another new type of beer can was introduced in 1940. Crown Cork and
Seal Company's can used a bottle cap like a cone top, but was shaped a bit
differently. Nicknamed "Silver Bumpers" because of their aluminum coating,

"All Aboard!" This
great locomotive
motion sign is
from Pabst
Brewing Company
of Milwaukee.

they were adopted by a rather small number of brewers. But they became the only cans available to the domestic U.S. market during World War II since they were made of (unrationed) cold-rolled steel.

World War II had a profound effect on the brewing industry. A number of American breweries profited from government contracts to provide beer for the military. Olive-drab cans even were rolled out for the armed forces. Due to material rationing, some struggling breweries were bought by competitors and closed, purchased just for their grain allotments. Other smaller breweries actually profited from the wartime shortages of beer. Wholesale outlets often were eager to pay them illegal money under the table in order to obtain beer. But for most of these small brewers, prosperity was destined to be short-lived.

World War II shortages also increased the use of quart bottles (to save the metal used for crowns) and brought about the manufacture for taverns of "composition" signs—advertising pieces made of compressed paper, foil, and a variety of substances only a chemist could identify.

While the world breathed a sigh of relief when the war finally ended, the brewing business was poised to undergo tremendous change. Expansion plans that had been put on hold were put back on the drawing board, and some ambitious American brewers were ready to become regional and even national powerhouses. Under this environment, marketing and branding became even more important factors in a brewery's success. The difference

Because of its durable aluminum coating, "Silver Bumpers" or Crowntainer-type cans, like this Neuweiler's of Allentown, Pennsylvania, often are found in good condition.

During World War II, beer cans, like this Schaefer from F&M Schaefer, New York, were painted olive drab for drinking in war zones—no shiny reflective surfaces to alert the enemy.

This World War II coaster printed by Blue Top Brewing, of Kitchener, Canada, urged its customers to "Buy Victory Bonds."

This composition sign, from the John Hohenadel Brewery of Philadelphia, had a mounting bracket on its back for wall hanging.

between their products was minimal, so the need to distinguish their beers via advertising became paramount.

In addition to point-of-purchase, billboard, and newspaper advertising, the use of magazine, radio, and television ads took off after the war. As the larger breweries began flexing their advertising muscles, small brewers found it more difficult to compete. By 1950, only about four hundred breweries were operating in the United States. Over the next decade, that number would be nearly halved.

One popular form of breweriana produced during the postwar decades was cardboard signs. Some of these signs were designed to be framed or tacked on a wall; others were "self-framed," with a border designed to look like a frame built into the cardboard.

The use of back-bar statues also grew during the 1950s. They often are referred to as "chalks," since a majority of them were made of plaster of Paris reinforced by things like chemicals, horsehair, and internal rods. Others were fabricated from a variety of materials including rubber, metal, plastic, and *papier mâché*. Back-bar pieces ranged from a couple of inches to a couple of feet tall and came in many different shapes. Some of the most popular chalks were figural, featuring such brewery icons as Sir John Falstaff and the flute-playing Johnny Pfeiffer. Many were designed to incorporate a bottle or a can, sometimes held aloft by a life-sized hand.

Crafted using soft-rubber production molds and hand-painted, such tavern displays are known to have been made by more than twenty-five different companies, with the two largest being Plasto Manufacturing

Opposite: "My Man's Brand" reads this self-framed cardboard sign from Red Top Brewing of Cincinnati, Ohio.

Company of Chicago and W. J. Smith Company of Louisville, Kentucky. Although colorful and impressive, chalks also are easily damaged, and it is not unlikely for existing statues to have been repaired (either poorly or impressively, depending on the craftsman).

In addition to chalks, the use of plastic in beer lights and signs also took off during this time. Other period pieces

Left: This detailed painted rubber statute of the Miller High Life girl was designed for display on a tavern's back bar.

Below: During the years that Pfeiffer Brewing of Detroit stressed its Johnny Pfeiffer character, as seen in this chalk piece, the company's sales more than doubled.

Foam scrapers also were known in their day by a popular nickname: "beer combs."

include foam scrapers, used by bartenders to push the foam off beer glasses and pitchers. These were used until the government deemed them unsanitary. Some brewers even had fancy holders made for their scrapers. Salt and pepper shakers designed as miniature beer bottles continued to be popular, as did bottle and can openers, the production of which was more than 200 million annually during the period. Smoking also was still a popular habit, and brewers continued to use matchbooks as an advertising device. They also put their names on glass ashtrays and on butane lighters when they became popular.

The 1950s saw a significant change in the design of beer labels. Beginning in 1950, a tax statement ("Internal Revenue Tax Paid" or something similar) no longer had to be included on bottles or cans. Although this left more room for a design, ironically it was during the decade that most labels became less ornate and much simpler.

Colorado brewer Adolph Coors Company introduced the first aluminum beer can in 1959. Three years later, the "tab top" can, which did not require an opener, was debuted by the Pittsburgh Brewing Company. That same year, the Theodore Hamm Brewing Company brought out the first can composed entirely of aluminum. By the end of the 1960s, canned beer was outselling bottled and draft beer for the first time in history.

The late 1960s also marked the beginning of what would become a nearly complete domination of the U.S. brewing industry by a few national brewing giants. The Anheuser-Busch Brewing Company led the way. The product of leading breweries also became further homogenized; most brewers didn't even bother to produce a bock beer any more.

Fewer breweries also meant fewer producers of breweriana, but curiously the hobby of collecting it was about to explode in popularity.

Hamm Brewing of St. Paul, Minneapolis, introduced the first all-aluminum beer can in America in 1962.

Bi-monthly Magazine for the Beer Can Collectors of America®

Beer Cans

& Brewery Collectibles

The story of
Champagne Velvet
Beer

CV
for me!

BEER BUZZ: 1970s–2000s

O BVIOUSLY, at least some people were interested in saving breweriana before Prohibition; otherwise none of it would still be around! Collectors are known to have started collecting breweriana as early as the 1930s. But these hobbyists were slow to organize themselves, most preferring to keep their collections "in the closet."

Probably the first group formed by collectors was the British Beermat Collectors Society, organized in 1960. Two clubs were organized in the United States in 1970: the Beer Can Collectors of America (BCCA), later renamed the Brewery Collectibles Club of America, and the Eastern Coast Breweriana Association (ECBA). Two years later came the National Association of Breweriana Advertising (NABA), started in the Midwest like the BCCA. Next came the American Breweriana Association, started in Colorado in 1980.

Some of the breweries in America were busy reorganizing themselves at this time as well. In 1970, the Miller Brewing Company of Milwaukee was purchased by tobacco giant Philip Morris. A couple years later, Miller acquired the obscure Meister Brau Lite brand name from a closed Chicago brewery.

Backed by Philip Morris's money, Miller proceeded to launch an advertising war with Anheuser-Busch. The renamed "Lite" brand propelled Miller into second place in U.S. beer production in 1977, and it was actually within shouting distance of Anheuser-Busch, closing the sales gap to about 10 million barrels in 1978. But Miller would fail to get any closer, and by 1984, Anheuser-Busch controlled more than one third of the U.S. market.

Light beers began to dominate this market, as indeed they still do. With a low alcohol content and around a hundred calories per twelve-ounce serving, light beers were met with acceptance by a huge portion of the American beer drinking public. As a result, even nonlight brands grew increasingly bland. As a former brewmaster for Coors would later put it, the beers that grew to dominate the American market offered little flavor other than that of yeast.

Opposite:
*Beer Cans and
Brewery Collectibles*
magazine is the
bimonthly
publication of the
largest breweriana
collecting club, the
BCCA.

The choice was getting a little bland for breweriana, too. The use of chalks and cardboard signs had dwindled, and the production of trays declined as well. Mirrors remained fairly popular, and a lot of cheap plastic signs and lights were churned out. Inexpensive plastic and paper calendars with tear-away numbers were likewise

Above:
A tap handle advertising Miller Brewing's Lite brand—the "Tastes Great, Less Filling" beer.

Above right:
Although made of inexpensive plastic, this "light up" from the Schlitz Brewing Company of Milwaukee is still an appealing sign when lit.

Right:
Plastic signs can be attractive, as illustrated by this colorful Knickerbocker sign distributed by the Jacob Ruppert brewery in Orange, New Jersey.

popular. The fact of the matter is that breweries were too preoccupied with television advertising to bother sinking much money into tavern pieces.

Two exceptions were cans and steins, and they became the most popular collectibles of the era. By the mid-1970s, can collecting had reached such popularity that it could rightfully be called a fad. Countless children and teenagers became involved in the hobby, snatching up beer cans from ditches while out bicycling. More adventurous collectors young and old got out their shovels and dug older cans out of garbage dumps. The can collecting craze reached its apex in 1978, when membership in the BCCA reached nearly twelve thousand collectors.

Meanwhile, the containers themselves had been changing. In 1964, aluminum cans accounted for a mere 2 percent of the beer can market. Brewers recognized the advantages of using less heavy packaging, but the price of steel cans was still cheap. This price began rising, and advances in the production of aluminum cans rendered them even lighter in weight. By the late 1970s, aluminum began to dominate the market, and steel cans soon became obsolete.

Pittsburgh Brewing of Pennsylvania honored the hometown Steelers after the team won the Super Bowl in 1975.

For collectors, the only good thing about aluminum cans was their resistance to rust. Paint did not take to them as well as it did to steel, making the artwork on the package less visually appealing. They also were easy to dent, and their light weight made them feel somehow less significant.

As beer can collecting grew in popularity in the mid-1970s, breweries recognized that they might be able to sell more beer by issuing special cans. Numerous brewers issued commemorative cans in 1976 in honor of the U.S. bicentennial. The practice took off from there.

The Pittsburgh Brewing Company sold beer in cans honoring local landmarks and sports teams; the August Schell Brewing Company of New Ulm, Minnesota, churned out cans for countless small-town celebrations; and the G. Heileman Brewing Company put its Sterling brand in fifteen different cans honoring winners of the Kentucky Derby.

Production of these special cans caused many collectors of newly released cans to reach

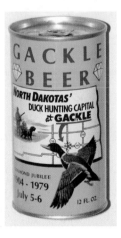

For those wanting to attend the 1979 celebration in Gackle, North Dakota, Schell Brewing, of New Ulm, Minnesota, conveniently provided a map on its commemorative can of the event.

Just one in a series of Budweiser Clydesdales Holiday mugs, issued by Anheuser-Busch.

something of a saturation point. Hobbyists began questioning the necessity of acquiring all the different colors of the Andy's or Bob's Special brand beer cans.

Despite the growing disinterest in special cans, breweriana collectors had a lot to be excited about in the 1970s. In 1975, Anheuser-Busch produced the first of what would become a wide-ranging offering of ceramic steins. The brewery's popular annual holiday stein series began in 1980. Other brewers hopped on board and began offering annual steins and/or mugs as well. Although some were cheaply produced, most of them were well crafted and produced by famous companies like Ceramarte of Brazil.

Many breweries took a nostalgic turn with some of their 1970s advertising items, a lot of them featuring images of women. The Olympia Brewing Company of Washington issued print reproductions of images of female models featured on some of its pre-Prohibition calendars. Anheuser-Busch made posters and trays based on its seventy-five-year-old "Budweiser Girls" designs. Schlitz dusted off its old girl atop-the-world icon for various pieces, including wall sconces and a giant lighted plastic sculpture. Miller returned some emphasis to its "Girl on the Moon" symbol, though her new outfit was a far cry from the original saucy circus performer who wore thick, colorful stockings and brandished a whip.

Any discussion of 1970s breweriana collecting would be incomplete without mentioning a famous name in canned beer: Billy. Introduced in 1977 amidst much fanfare and named after Billy Carter, the miscreant brother of

Miller Brewing Company reintroduced its "Girl on the Moon" advertising theme in the 1970s, as prominently displayed on this tip tray.

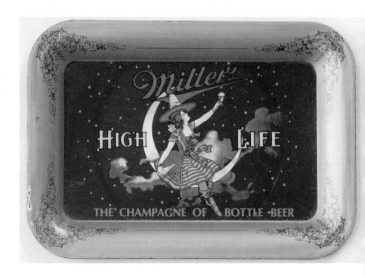

then-U.S. President Jimmy Carter, Billy Beer was produced by several breweries throughout the country. But, it proved to be short lived. Tons of people saved Billy cans in the mistaken belief that they some day would be worth a lot of money. Collectors then and now scoff at anyone willing to pay a penny for them.

The Carter family would end up having a bigger role in the beer business than the Billy brand when brother Jimmy signed legislation legalizing home brewing. From the efforts of these home brewers would spring a brewing revolution.

A full six-pack of Billy beer cans. These cans are not valuable, contrary to popular belief.

The same year that Billy beer was introduced, Jack McAuliffe began selling beer made at his New Albion Brewing Company in Sonoma, California. This is considered the first "microbrewery" in the United States, a tag applied to any brewery with a production of fewer than fifteen thousand barrels a year. Bert Grant opened the first U.S. brewpub (a term used to designate a brewery that sells its own beer on premise and frequently serves food as well), Grant's Brewery Pub, in 1982 in Yakima, Washington.

These two businesses were barely a blip on the beer radar screen at the time. Not counting Prohibition, the number of brewing companies in the United States had reached the lowest point in at least 150 years by 1983, when only 51 brewing concerns operated around 80 manufacturing plants. The top six brewers in the country controlled 92 percent of the market.

The American brewing industry ended the decade with Anheuser-Busch accounting for 43.7 percent of domestic beer sales. It had become the first brewer to ever exceed an annual production mark of 80 million barrels. The

A Stout label from the first microbrewery: New Albion Brewing, Sonoma, California. (Courtesy of George S. Akin.)

decade also ended with a kick in the teeth and the necessity for brewers to have to change all their labels, when teetotaling Senator Strom Thurmond of South Carolina and other assorted do-gooders succeeded in getting the government to mandate that a statement be placed on all containers of alcoholic beverage warning consumers of the possible dangers of drinking. The law became effective on November 18, 1989.

The 1990s saw a continued renaissance of the craft brewing movement that started to take off in the previous decade. By 1994, California alone had more breweries in operation than there had been in the entire United States just a decade earlier. This led to a revolution in breweriana collecting as well, for hobbyists now had items from a growing number of small breweries to collect.

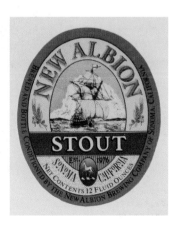

An IPA label from Copper Dragon of Carbondale, Illinois. Although shuttered for only a few years, breweriana from this brewpub is already scarce.

Cans and bottles from six different microbreweries, showing the colorful designs typical of these labels.

Although the new small breweries concentrated most of their efforts on brewing fuller-flavored beer, they also produced various types of breweriana. Brewpubs are an especially friendly setting for such items as coasters, napkins, and glasses. Tap knobs are another way for small brewers to express themselves. Attention-getting knobs of an array of shapes and sizes were demanded by the craft brewers to try to catch the attention of tavern-goers. Manufacturers responded to their call with designs in plastic, wood, metal, and other substances.

The microbrewing revolution also brought back a venerable American tradition: "rushing the growler." This colorful term refers to a practice that dated from the pre-Prohibition days in which patrons brought their own containers to local breweries and taverns. There they were filled with draft beer that was taken home to be consumed. Use of growlers was common in various parts of the United States, and children often were used as couriers (no doubt they often were tempted to try a sip on the way home). Various containers were used for growlers, but it was usually just a metal pail, several of which could be looped over a broomstick to allow a pair of youngsters to transport multiple buckets.

The growler tradition includes possibly apocryphal tales of bartenders holding the containers far from the tap while pouring, which would create a lot of foam and result in the customer getting less beer. Patrons allegedly responded to this problem by coating the growler with butter to keep the foam down. The term "growler" is said to come from the noise made by the customer as he reacted to seeing how little beer was actually in the container as he was leaving the tavern.

Although a few breweries issued glass growlers featuring their logos into the 1960s, thereafter the practice all but ended until the brewpubs came along. Today's growlers typically are standard-shaped glass containers holding a half-gallon of beer and are equipped with a finger-hole for easy carrying. They almost always feature the brewery name and logo and are therefore highly collectible, if a bit bulky.

Stein collectors continued to see the larger breweries produce annual and other mugs and steins (a mug is simply a stein without a lid) through the 1980s. In 1995, the Anheuser-Busch Collectors Club began offering an annual members-only stein. Steins with sports themes, military themes, and themes based on advertising characters like the Hamm's bear and the Bud Man were produced.

This finely detailed stein, issued by Anheuser-Busch and featuring a portrait of Adolphus Busch is a 1990s reproduction of one created in the 1890s. (Courtesy of Bill Cress).

This growler once was filled with the fresh brews of Hermann Brewing, Hermann, Missouri. Sadly, this fine brewpub closed in the early 2000s.

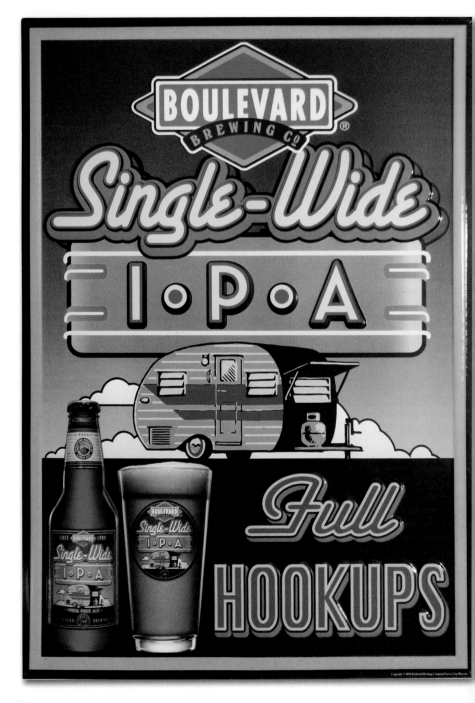

Collectors eventually began to see the market become a bit saturated, just like can collectors had in the 1970s. As the value of some steins continued to rise, fakes began appearing on the market. Though they are still a popular collectible, the stein craze has receded, as symbolized by the demise of the Anheuser-Busch Collectors Club in 2007.

Anheuser-Busch Brewing Company, meanwhile, continued to dominate the market. It had completed construction of its thirteenth United States brewery in Cartersville, Georgia, in 1993, at which time its domestic market share stood at 44.3 percent. Its net income for the year was just less than $1 billion. Corporate brass had long dreamed of reaching the point where Anheuser-Busch sold half the beer in the United States, but the closest it ever got was in 2003 when it controlled 49.8 percent of the market. Since then, its share has slowly shrunk.

Many brewpubs and microbreweries came and went in the 1990s and beyond. Breweriana from many of the shorter-lived ones is extremely rare. Other craft brewers such as Samuel Adams and Sierra Nevada saw their sales grow so great that they could scarcely be called micros.

Since most small brewers sell their products strictly on-premise, they therefore have little need for point-of-purchase advertising. But these larger producers began shipping their products far and wide, so found the need to have various styles of signs made. Such pieces range from thin metal "tackers" (so lightweight that they can be hung using tacks pushed through small holes on the signs' corners) to mirrors, and from "flange" signs (used also before Prohibition and hung from a wall on a brace) to colorful neons.

The smaller brewers have taken delight in producing a huge variety of beers and also have used great imagination when it comes to naming the brands and designing the labels for their bottles. In addition, to respond to the growth of the craft beer portion of the market, the larger brewers began producing new brands and styles of their own, leading to a further increase in available breweriana.

While the growth of the microbrewery segment of the industry was taking place, the giant national brewers were battling over their huge share of the market, as the big outfits continued to get bigger. By 1993, there were just five major players in United States brewing. Anheuser-Busch sold 87.3 million barrels that year, nearly twice as

Opposite: This colorful metal "tacker" was distributed in 2010 by Boulevard Brewing, of Kansas City, Missouri, to promote the introduction of its Single Wide IPA brand.

A paperweight issued by Anheuser-Busch commemorating the brewery's first 100-million-barrel production year.

An applied label pint glass for Samuel Adams beer, issued by the Boston Beer Company of Boston, Massachusetts.

much as its nearest competitor, Miller. The Adolph Coors Company of Colorado was third at nearly 20 million barrels, followed by Stroh of Detroit and the Lacrosse, Wisconsin-based Heileman. Once-mighty competitors like Schlitz and Falstaff had fallen by the wayside.

In 2001, Anheuser-Busch became the first brewing company in history to produce the staggering total of 100 million barrels of beer in a single year. Miller sales had shrunk to just more than 40 million barrels, while that of Coors had increased to nearly 23 million. Stroh had acquired Heileman and was in turn bought by Pabst, whose sales for the year totaled fewer than 10 million

Issued around the year 2000, this back-bar light-up Tetley's Bitter sign, from the Tetley Brewery in Leeds, England, was made to look old.

barrels. Pabst would end up becoming a "virtual" brewer, without any operating breweries of its own, its many brands farmed out to other brewers, primarily Miller in Milwaukee.

Rounding out the top five U.S. brewers in 2001 was the Boston Beer Company. Its Samuel Adams brand, based on a pre-Prohibition formula, accounted for 1.1 million barrels, further pushing the envelope in deciding what the definition of a microbrewer should be.

The first decade of the twenty-first century saw further consolidation among the industry giants, this time with an international flair. In 2002, Miller merged with global brewing powerhouse SAB (South African Breweries, which originated in nineteenth-century South Africa) to form SAB-Miller. Then, in 2005, Coors merged with the Molson brewing group of Canada. Two years later, Molson-Coors and SAB-Miller combined their U.S. brewing operations. The formation of Miller-Coors meant that just two brewing concerns, it and Anheuser-Busch, controlled 80 percent of the U.S. market.

In 2007, Anheuser-Busch began serving as the U.S. distributor for InBev, which had been formed in 2004 as a combination of Brazilian and Belgian brewing interests, the latter with roots in fourteenth-century Belgium. Among its brands were Beck's, Stella Artois, and Bass Ale. Rumors soon began swirling of an InBev/Anheuser-Busch merger, which culminated in InBev acquiring all the outstanding shares of Anheuser-Busch stock in a $52-billion deal in 2008.

Although of interest to investors, these corporate shenanigans had little impact on collectors of breweriana. The combined brewers continued churning out plenty of advertising items for their various brands. Old stand-bys like mirrors and tackers remained plentiful, and the early twenty-first century has become something of a golden era for neon signs. The two mega-brewers, and many of the smaller ones, are producing many colorful neons, some of them quite large. They also are experimenting with LED displays as an alternative to neon tubing.

A Wheat Beer aluminum bottle from Boulevard Brewing of Kansas City. Some collectors have nicknamed this container a "cabottle."

Some craft brewers also are starting to can their beers, producing renewed interest in that aspect of the breweriana collecting hobby. Aluminum bottles likewise have recently aroused the interest of collectors.

Although U.S. beer sales have been flat or worse for the international behemoths, the craft brewing segment of the beer industry, though still less than 5 percent of the total annual 200 million barrel market, has continued its steady growth. The first half of 2010 saw an estimated increase in craft

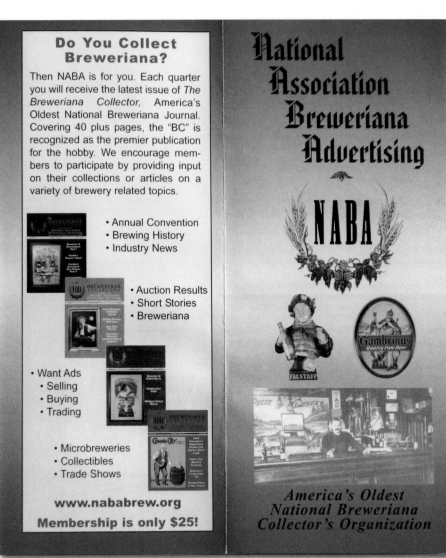

beer sales of 9 percent, while overall U.S. sales plummeted nearly 3 percent. The market for fuller flavored beers, and a corresponding brewpub culture, have become firmly established, despite the fact that six out of the top ten best-selling beers in the United States continue to contain the word "light" (or in the case of Miller's leading seller, "lite").

In addition to the many brands of the brewing industry giants, some of the older brands of beer and their corresponding breweriana are still being produced. A few of the regional breweries, such as Yuengling, Schell, Stevens Point, and Lion, still survive, and new brewpubs and microbreweries are opening nearly every day.

As the third millennium enters its second decade, the previous one hundred fifty years have seen the industry come full circle. Once again the majority of Americans live close to a brewery, where they can sample beers that have traveled only a very short distance from the brew kettle to their lips.

Where the brewing industry goes from here is anybody's guess. A prognosticator surveying the brewing scene in 1880 would have been hard pressed to forecast either national Prohibition or the disappearance of small brewers from the scene. How could brewers in the age of horse-drawn delivery wagons ever have foreseen the possibility of a single company producing nearly half the beer consumed in the United States?

Nor could a customer standing in the middle of a liquor store in 1975, scanning the shelves for available beers (and finding almost all of them to be pale lagers with names that had been around for decades) ever have imagined the huge variety of beers that would be available thirty or forty years later.

It would be equally difficult to predict the future of the breweriana collecting hobby, although it undoubtedly will continue to exist in some form. When it comes to many of the older collectibles, hobbyists find themselves fighting a constant battle against deterioration. Even under carefully controlled temperature and humidity conditions, items will slowly fade away. Of course, this will make the older breweriana that stays in nice condition even more desirable.

Collectors themselves also face preservation issues. Though many younger folks certainly are interested in breweriana and beer, most of the dedicated collectors are getting up in years. Where will their collections go after they are no longer around?

As the breweriana collecting clubs and other social organizations can attest, it is difficult to attract the younger generations to their fold. But while it may not be easy, it should not be impossible for the hobby to attract followers. Such colorful and interesting collectibles, connected with an industry with a fascinating history, a dynamic present, and what is sure to be an interesting future, are sure to attract devotees.

Opposite: This membership application is from the National Association of Breweriana Advertising (NABA), a club that actively recruits collectors of all types of breweriana.

PLACES TO VISIT

Most breweries offer guided tours of their facilities, and in addition to gift shops, many of them feature breweriana displays. A lot of the bigger breweries have regularly scheduled tours, while most of the smaller ones will be happy to show visitors around with (or even without) advance notice. Some of these breweries—large and small—include Anchor Brewing Company in San Francisco; Anheuser-Busch in St. Louis; Coors Brewery in Golden, Colorado; Flying Dog Brewery in Frederick, Maryland; Rogue Ales in Newport, Oregon; The Boston Beer (Samuel Adams) Company brewery in Boston; and Wynkoop Brewing Co. in Denver.

Tourists with an eye for viewing larger displays of breweriana would be well advised to visit some of the museums dedicated to the subject, including The National Brewery Museum and The World of Beer Memorabilia Museum.

THE NATIONAL BREWERY MUSEUM
The National Brewery Museum was conceived by the American Breweriana Association in 1982, when Stan Galloway, the group's leader, inserted into its articles of incorporation the goal of "a non-commercial museum of brewing history and advertising." Two years later, the club voted to start a museum fund by donating any profits derived from its annual meetings into the fund. In 2003, the ABA elected to partner with the Potosi Brewery

Inside one of the larger display rooms at the American Breweriana Association's National Brewery Museum in Potosi, Wisconsin. (Courtesy John Dutcher, ABA Museum.)

This display in the ABA National Brewery Museum is filled with rare breweriana from the breweries in Dubuque, Iowa. (Courtesy John Dutcher, ABA Museum.)

Foundation, which had the idea of creating a museum and restoring the town's closed brewery to house it. The Potosi Brewing Company, established in the 1850s, had closed in 1972. On June 19, 2008, a grand opening was held for the National Brewery Museum and Research Library in the fully restored brewery.

The museum features impressive permanent displays of all types of breweriana, plus numerous rotating displays set up by collectors. Even veterans of the collecting hobby are impressed by the quality of the exhibits. The museum includes a research library for visitors seeking historical information. In addition there is a brewpub on site, providing food and fresh beer that can be enjoyed before and/or after touring the museum, which is open year-round.

The National Brewery Museum
209 S. Main Street
Potosi, WI 53820
http://nationalbrewerymuseum.org

THE WORLD OF BEER MEMORABILIA MUSEUM

The ABA published a special commemorative issue of its magazine celebrating the 2008 opening of the National Brewery Museum. In this issue appeared an ad from the Minhas Craft Brewery, seeking any breweriana associated with that brewery and its predecessors. The ad also solicited donations of breweriana for the brewery's museum, located in its gift and tour center.

Sadly, of the Wisconsin breweries represented in this case at the National Brewery Museum, none is still in business. (Courtesy John Dutcher, ABA Museum.)

Minhas is located in Monroe, Wisconsin, about seventy miles west of Potosi. Brewing on the site dates from 1845, and for many years it was the property of the Joseph Huber Brewing Company. It acquired the Minhas name in 2006 when the struggling brewery was purchased by Ravinder Minhas, a young businessman whose Mountain Crest Beverage Company in Western Canada had used Huber as a contract brewer.

Minhas's 2008 plea for museum donations bore considerable fruit just two years later with the establishment in the brewery's visitor center of the World of Beer Memorabilia Museum, also known as the Haydock Museum.

Herb and Helen Haydock pose in front of a 1928 Chevy beer delivery truck at the Minhas World of Beer Memorabilia Museum, in Monroe, Wisconsin. (Courtesy Tami Hoesly, Minhas Museum.)

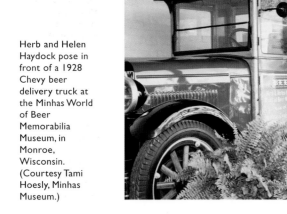

The museum's displays consist of part of the giant collection of breweriana amassed by collecting stalwarts Herb and Helen Haydock, a married couple and natives of Wisconsin, who started collecting in the 1950s.

The museum houses an incredible variety of breweriana in three separate rooms, all of which are filled from floor to ceiling with advertising items. Two of the rooms are devoted to antique advertising; the third is dedicated to microbreweries and even has displays on the ceiling. Visitors also are invited to take a tour of the brewery and visit the Minhas gift and exhibit area.

Minhas Craft Brewery & Haydock Museum, 1208 Brewery (14th) Avenue, Monroe, WI 53566

Website: www.minhasbrewery.com

Above:
This pre-Prohibition "Pabst Yard Girl" lithograph from Pabst Brewing of Milwaukee, Wisconsin, measures 36 inches long.

Left:
This display at the Minhas Museum in Monroe, Wisconsin, features the Hamm's bear. (Both photos courtesy Tami Hoesly, Minhas Museum.)

55

INDEX

Page numbers in Italics refer to
illustrations.